MY STOMPIN' GROUNDS

and four other songs

STOMPIN' TOM CONNORS

illustrations by
KURT SWINGHAMMER

Doubleday Canada Limited

Copyright © 1992 by Crown-Vetch Music Limited (a division of Stompin' Tom Limited)
Copyright © 1992 by Kurt Swinghammer (illustrations)

"The Hockey Song," "Cross Canada," "Canada Day, Up Canada Way," and "Unity" lyrics by Tom C. Connors © Crown-Vetch Music Limited (a division of Stompin' Tom Limited) and used by permission.

"My Stompin' Grounds" lyrics by Tom C. Connors and Roy A. Payne © Crown-Vetch Music Limited and Morning Music Limited and used by permission.

All rights reserved. No part of this publication may be reproduced, stored in a retrieval system, or transmitted, in any form or by any means, electronic, mechanical, photocopying, recording or otherwise, without the prior written permission of Doubleday Canada Limited.

CANADIAN CATALOGUING IN PUBLICATION DATA

Connors, Stompin' Tom, 1936–
    My stompin' grounds

ISBN 0-385-25406-7

I. Swinghammer, Kurt, 1957– . II. Title.

PS8555.O666M9 1992   jC811'.54   C92–094987-8
PZ8.3.C66My 1992

Designed by Tania Craan
Printed and bound in Canada by Metropole Litho, Quebec

Published in Canada by
Doubleday Canada Limited
105 Bond Street
Toronto, Ontario
M5B 1Y3

MY STOMPIN' GROUNDS

Just take a little piece of P.E.I. and old Saskatchewan,
Nova Scotia and New Brunswick, Quebec and
    Newfoundland;
Alberta and Manitoba, Ontario and B.C.,
And you'll have found the Stompin' Grounds of all my
    friends and me,
And you'll have found the Stompin' Grounds of all my
    friends and me.

I've been all across this country,
From the east coast to the west;
And I've been asked about a thousand times,
What places I liked best;

Well, I've had to base my answers
On the friendly people I've found;
And, if you're inclined to take the time,
This is where you'll find my Stompin' Grounds.

There was a time, with a buddy of mine,
When a freight train was our abode;
And we found people in this here land,
That would help a guy along the road;

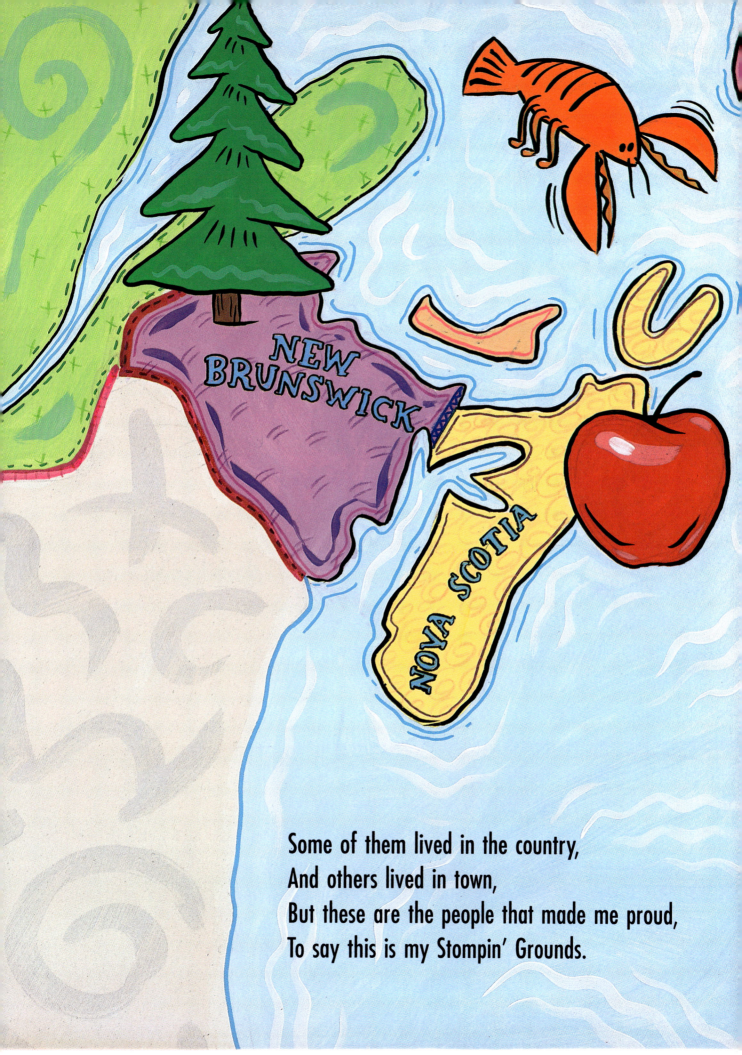

Some of them lived in the country,
And others lived in town,
But these are the people that made me proud,
To say this is my Stompin' Grounds.

And now you've heard my answer;
It's one I hope you'll understand;
It's just my way of saying "thank you"
To the people of this land;

And it doesn't matter, really, where you're from,
You can spread the word around;
Where ever you find a heart that's kind,
You're in a part of my Stompin' Grounds.

Cross Canada

C-A-N-A-D-A,
Tell me what's a Douglas Fir?

C-A-N-A-D-A,
Bet you never heard a bobcat purr;

C-A-N-A-D-A, Have you ever seen a lobster crawl?
In Canada, we get to see them all.

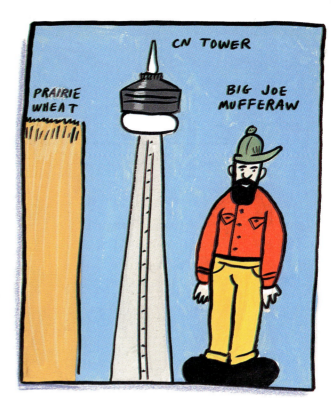

We get to see the Maple trees,
Maple sugar and the Maple leaves;

We've got the biggest wheat fields growin' tall

In Canada, where we see the reversing falls;
In Canada, we get to see them all.

C-A-N-A-D-A, Tell me what's a tidal bore?
C-A-N-A-D-A, Have you ever heard the ocean roar?

C-A-N-A-D-A,
Just listen to the wild goose call;

In Canada, we get to see them all.

We get to see the Maple trees,
Maple sugar and the Maple leaves;

We've got the biggest timber woods so tall;

In Canada, where adventure ever calls;

In Canada, we get to see them all.

C-A-N-A-D-A,
Have you ever heard a Maple Creek?

C-A-N-A-D-A,
Bet you never seen a mountain peak;

C-A-N-A-D-A, In the land of the big snow ball;
In Canada, we get to see them all.

C-A-N-A-D-A,
Have you ever seen a magnetic hill?

C-A-N-A-D-A,
Or a lady on a dollar bill?

C-A-N-A-D-A,
Bet you never seen the autumn fall;

In Canada, we get to see them all.

It's Canada Day, up Canada way, on the first day of July,
And we're shoutin' hurray! up Canada way,
When the Maple Leaf flies high;
When the silver jets from east to west go streaming
    through our sky,
We'll be shoutin' hurray! up Canada way,
When the great parade goes by.

O Canada, standing tall together
We raise our hands and hail our flag, the Maple
    Leaf forever.

It's Canada Day, up Canada way, on the coast of Labrador;
And we're shoutin' hurray! up Canada way,
On the wide Pacific shore;
People everywhere have a song to share on Canada's holiday,
From Pelee Island in the sunny south to the North Pole far away;

It's Canada Day, up Canada way, when the long cold winter's done;
And we're shoutin' hurray! up Canada way, for the great days yet to come;
Where Maple trees grow Maple leaves when the northern sun is high;
We're Canadians and we're born again on the first day of July.

It's Canada Day, up Canada way, from the lakes to the
   prairies wide;
And we're shoutin' hurray! up Canada way, on the
   St. Lawrence side,
People everywhere have a song to share on Canada's holiday,
From Pelee Island in the sunny south to the North Pole far away.

the HOCKEY SONG

Hello out there, we're on the air, it's hockey night tonight.
Tension grows, the whistle blows and the puck goes down the ice.

Oh, the good old hockey game is the best game you can name;

And the best game you can name is the good old hockey game.

Second period …
Where players dash with skates a-flash, the home team trails behind;
But they grab the puck and go bursting up and they're down across the line;

They storm the crease, like the bumble bees,
They travel like a burning flame;
We see them slide the puck inside,
It's a 1–1 hockey game.

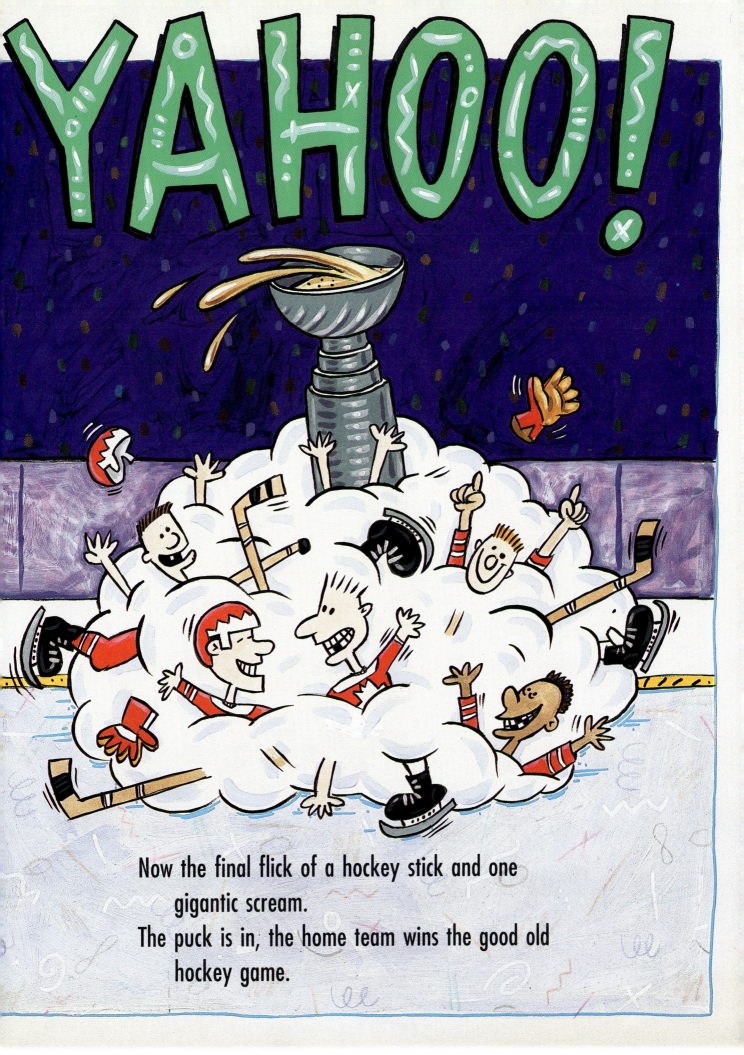

Now the final flick of a hockey stick and one gigantic scream.
The puck is in, the home team wins the good old hockey game.

Unity for you is unity for me;
Unity for all means all for unity.
Together we shall rise forever to recall
That the Maple tree is unity, and our flag will never fall.

When I was just a child I had a wondrous dream,
I travelled through a land where freedom was supreme;
Rising in the north and stretching sea to sea,
Where the voices rang and people sang a song of unity.

Someone said to come and took me by the hand,
And opened up my eyes to the blessings of the land;
Nature was in bloom with abundance everywhere,
Then I hear those magic words come ringing through the air.

Then I saw the flag, a Maple Leaf unfurled,
Standing on a tower, the highest in the world.
And as I watched it wave, its colours came in view;
The red was sacred brotherhood and the white was pure and true.

One small Maple Leaf was pinned to my lapel,
Then the dream did end, but I still remember well,
The voice that said to write and sing of what shall be,
There's a promised land for those who stand in
Canada's unity.